CW01335664

THE COMMUN...
WE CALL CHURCH

An Introduction for RCIA

Hans Christoffersen

Liguori

Imprimi Potest:
Stephen T. Rehrauer, CSsR, Provincial
Denver Province
The Redemptorists

Imprimatur: "In accordance with CIC 827, permission to publish has been granted on May 21, 2018, by the Most Reverend Mark S. Rivituso, Auxiliary Bishop, Archdiocese of St. Louis. Permission to publish is an indication that nothing contrary to Church teaching is contained in this work. It does not imply any endorsement of the opinions expressed in the publication; nor is any liability assumed by this permission."

Copyright © 2018, 2002 Liguori Publications

ISBN 978-0-7648-2807-2

All rights reserved. No part of this publication may be reproduced, stored in a retrieval system, or transmitted in any form or by any means— electronic, mechanical, photocopy, recording, or any other—except for brief quotations in printed reviews, without the prior written permission of Liguori Publications.

Scripture quotations are from the *New Revised Standard Version of the Bible*, copyright © 1989 by the Division of Christian Education of the National Council of Churches of Christ in the USA. Used with permission. All rights reserved.

Excerpts from the English translation of the *Catechism of the Catholic Church* for use in the United States of America copyright © 1994, United States Catholic Conference, Inc.—*Libreria Editrice Vaticana*. English translation of the *Catechism of the Catholic Church: Modifications from the Editio Typica* copyright © 1997 United States Catholic Conference, Inc.—*Libreria Editrice Vaticana*. Used with permission.

Selections from *The Basic Sixteen Documents Vatican Council II*; General Editor, Austin Flannery, OP (Costello Publishing Company, New York, 1996), are used with permission.

Cover design: John Krus
Cover photo: CNS/Gregory A. Shemitz

To order, call 1-800-325-9521, or visit Liguori.org.

Printed in the United States of America
22 21 20 19 18 / 5 4 3 2 1

BILL WITTMAN

INTRODUCTION

"I stopped into church for a few minutes on my way to the bus stop."

"She's a member of the Catholic Church."

"The Catholic Church has representation at the United Nations."

"The Church is one, holy, catholic, and apostolic."

"Did you light a candle in church today?"

When non-Catholics first inquire about the Catholic community of faith and hear the many ways in which Catholics use the word "church," it can be somewhat bewildering. The examples on page 3 make it clear that the word is used in distinctly different ways: a building with doors and windows; a religious organization; a "political" entity; a community and communion of believers. So when we talk about "church," we need to clarify the context in which we perceive and speak—often without words—about this dynamic "place" in our lives.

MIA STUDIO/SHUTTERSTOCK

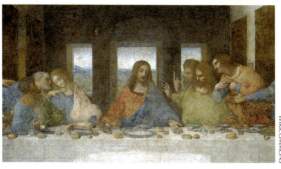

WIKICOMMONS

We need to do so among ourselves but especially to those who come to us interested in joining the catechumenate.

Most Christians are convinced that the Church can be traced back to Jesus Christ. This is true even though we are aware that the New Testament doesn't give us a precise and singular idea of what it means to be Church. But Jesus gave his disciples concepts and building blocks with which they could "build" a Church both strong and flexible enough to serve the good news of salvation until "the end of the ages" (1 Peter 1:20). As Catholics, we therefore believe there is a fundamental continuity between the Church of the New Testament and the Church of today.

IMAGES OF CHURCH

Let us look briefly at two of the most important images in which we, as Catholics, perceive ourselves as Church.

THE CHURCH AS THE BODY OF CHRIST

A case can be made that the Church was born at the Last Supper. As Jesus wished to join his disciples to himself, the Eucharist becomes that which unites us to one another and to Christ. This is what "Church" is: People bound together with each other and with Christ in Eucharist become the body of Christ. This concept is very strong in Paul's letters where our shared identification and participation in baptism, Eucharist, and the life of the Holy Spirit means that we are a new creation. "So if anyone is in Christ, there is a new creation: everything old has passed away; see, everything has become new!" (2 Corinthians 5:17).

Being "in Christ" so intimately means we are one with Christ in all we do: "The bread that we break, is it not a sharing in the body of Christ? Because there is one bread, we who are many are one body, for we all partake of the one bread" (1 Corinthians 10:16b–17). This image

of the Christian community is a mystical one—
the mystical body of Christ, of which Christ
himself is the head. As such, the Church is never
"somewhere else" or "someone else"; *we* make up
the Church.

THE CHURCH AS GOD'S PEOPLE

Being the body of Christ does not make the
Church identical to Christ. The Church is a
Church of sinners ever in need of conversion and
of becoming more conformed to the image of
Christ (Romans 8:29). An image of the Church
in its historical nature, limitation, and journey of
hope still lying ahead—an image besides that of
the body of Christ—is needed.

The First Letter of Peter addresses Christians
as "exiles…who have been chosen and destined
by God the Father and sanctified by the Spirit
to be obedient to Jesus Christ" (1 Peter 1:1–2a).
In the second chapter, the letter speaks of these
"scattered exiles" as a people—God's people:

> *But you are a chosen race, a royal priesthood,*
> *a holy nation, God's own people....Once you*
> *were not a people, but now you are God's*
> *people.*

> 1 PETER 2:9–10

This concept was not new. In the Book of Leviticus, God promises the Jews a covenant where "I will walk among you, and will be your God, and you shall be my people" (26:12), and the prophet Jeremiah says that this covenant is so important to God that "I will write it on their hearts; and I will be their God, and they shall be my people" (Jeremiah 31:33). The first Christians applied this concept to their new situation of seeing themselves as God's new pilgrim people journeying—growing "in the grace and knowledge of our Lord and Savior Jesus Christ" (2 Peter 3:18)—toward the fulfillment of Christian hope. The quote from the First Letter of Peter, above, also mentions the early Christians as a royal priesthood. Because of their shared experience of having been baptized into the passion, death, and resurrection of Christ, the early Christians saw themselves united in the dignity and the responsibility to participate in living and proclaiming God's good news in Christ.

There are other images of what it means to be Church in the New Testament writings: vineyard, sheepfold, the temple of the Lord, the temple of the Holy Spirit, etc. Common to all of them is that God's word is heard and kept alive in the

life of the Christian community. Faith and life in
Jesus Christ is in a community called together by
him and united to him; Christ is the root of its
existence.

LUKASZ SZWAJ/SHUTTERSTOCK

THE FORMATION OF CHRISTIAN COMMUNITY

The Acts of the Apostles gives us a sense of the earliest Christian community in Jerusalem. The time is right after the resurrection and ascension of Christ and the day of Pentecost:

> *Day by day, as they spent much time together in the temple, they broke bread at home and ate their food with glad and generous hearts, praising God and having the goodwill of all the people. And day by day the Lord added to their number those who were being saved.*
>
> ACTS OF THE APOSTLES 2:46–47

The first Christians went to the Temple and considered themselves a special group within Judaism. What was special to their Jewish community was the breaking of the bread—the Eucharist that bound them together with one another and with Christ. This they celebrated in their homes.

Only when Peter argued for baptizing Cornelius, a Roman centurion, were they compelled to reconsider their self-understanding in a more foundational way. This, however, was no easy transition. Did Gentile Christians first have to become Jews? Paul confronted Peter about this in Antioch. "If you, though a Jew, live like a Gentile and not like a Jew, how can you compel the Gentiles to live like Jews?" (Galatians 2:14b).

This led to the famous meeting of the apostles in Jerusalem. The apostles met within a larger group of believers from the Jerusalem community, and while Peter had a unique position of leadership, the discussion was open and candid. The question was considered in light "of all the signs and wonders that God had done through them among the Gentiles" (Acts 15:12) as well as in light of the Scriptures (see verses 15–18). At the end, the decision was made by "the apostles and the elders, with the consent of the whole church" (verse 22a). This meeting is important not only because of the actual decision, but also because of the formation of the new Christian community.

When the apostles communicated their decision, they did so convinced that they were aided in their decision by the Holy Spirit (see verse 28). Believing that the Holy Spirit guides the Church means that we trust that the Spirit of Christ leads our human efforts and our striving toward God's truth: "When the Spirit of truth comes, he will guide you into all the truth" (John 16:13a). On the day of Pentecost, the Holy Spirit transformed the earliest Christian community into a community gathered, strengthened, and sent in the mystery of the risen Christ.

In order to understand what it means, that Jesus Christ founded a Church gathered, strengthened, and sent in the mystery of the risen Christ, we must look closer at what Jesus did. Jesus spent his public ministry as an *itinerant* preacher. He healed the sick and called others to go and do the same: proclaim peace, heal the sick, and expel demons.

But there were other followers as well. Some stayed home and supported the preachers in their efforts. Examples of these are Martha and Mary and their brother Lazarus. These families and groups could very well have been the centers around which the local communities first arose. These communities were often founded

CNS/VICTOR ALEMAN

by these itinerant preachers—apostles—as in the examples of Paul and the companions with whom he traveled. They seemed to have done so with an "apostolic authority" that remained after they had moved on to other places.

On top of this apostolic foundation, the local communities seem to have formed their own organization and daily leadership structure, most often based on what they already knew. For the Jews, it was the local synagogue. For the Greeks, it was the *ekklésia*—the various local social associations. This is the word Paul used when he addressed the communities he had founded or intended to visit.

THE ROLE OF PETER

The New Testament doesn't present us with a uniform church structure. It isn't completely clear what organizational function "the Twelve" exercised—only Peter's unique position is singled out. In the Gospels, Peter is portrayed as the spokesman of the apostles, and in the Acts of the Apostles—after the resurrection—he definitely sees himself as such, a fact acknowledged and testified to by Paul.

That Catholics claim the papacy rests on the New Testament is based on two passages from the Gospel of Matthew that both deal with Jesus giving authority to bind and loose. In Matthew 16, the Lord gives this authority to Peter:

> *"And I tell you, you are Peter, and on this rock I will build my church, and the gates of Hades will not prevail against it. I will give you the keys of the kingdom of heaven, and whatever you bind on earth will be bound in heaven, and whatever you loose on earth will be loosed in heaven."*
>
> MATTHEW 16:18–19

GIULIO NAPOLITANO/SHUTTERSTOCK

Two chapters later, in Matthew 18:18, the same words and authority of Jesus are spoken and given to the Church as a whole: "Truly I tell you, whatever you bind on earth will be bound in heaven, and whatever you loose on earth will be loosed in heaven." When taken together, it leaves little doubt that the position of primacy fell to Peter—his human limitations notwithstanding. There is likewise little doubt that he relied on the broader community for guidance and correction in this charge given him by the Lord. The Church and its leadership was a communal enterprise, and Peter's role was from the beginning one of building bridges and binding together the local communities—what we believe to be the "one, holy, catholic, and apostolic Church" that we profess every Sunday.

A LITTLE HISTORY

In the decades following the apostles, the Christians developed the view that the communion they shared, gathered around the celebration of the mysteries (the sacraments, especially baptism and the Eucharist), was one in which the many local communities "put flesh and bones" on the one universal Church. In baptism, God promises God's people unity in the one faith in Christ the Lord: "one Lord, one faith, one baptism" (Ephesians 4:5). This oneness of faith takes the believers beyond place and time, and this is what is expressed in the Eucharist, where every celebration unites the local community to the universal Church and makes the universal Church present in every local celebration.

BILL WITTMAN

An expression of this profound "communion" among the churches was a custom of sending the consecrated bread out to other churches. On feast days in Rome, newly consecrated bread was sent to outlying communities where it was mixed into the wine in the chalice. When a priest today puts a small piece of the host into the chalice right before communion, it is a remnant of this tradition.

The way of expressing the liturgy and the theology of the ancient Church was varied and shaped by the cultural contexts and customs of various regions. The earliest and most important cities where Christianity grew—Jerusalem, Antioch, Alexandria, Rome, Milan, and Constantinople—became centers of learning, authoritative teaching, and administration. Of these, Rome, where both Peter and Paul were martyred, soon enjoyed a prominent position.

The merging of a Christian community founded by these two great apostles with the Roman predilection for efficiency, organization, structure, and legal orderliness made the papacy develop into an ever-stronger religious center, so that Pope Gregory the Great (590-604) could call himself "Servant of the Servants of God." At the same time, this Roman preference for the concrete also led to an emphasis on a more visible form of the unity of the Church, due in no small part to the deterioration of the political infrastructure of the western part of the Roman empire. As time went on, this led to an ever-greater, centralized view of the Church and a gradual loss of the value of diversity among the various regional customs and liturgical rites: the western Church became more and more identified with the Roman rite.

SECOND VATICAN COUNCIL RENEWAL

Saint John XXIII surprised the whole world when he announced his intention to call a worldwide council of the Church. Prior to that day in 1959, church councils had been called to respond to crises in the Church such as heresies or threatening divisions. Saint John called the Second Vatican Council to prepare the Church for a new millennium of witness and evangelization. Perhaps because of the surprise, it was popular to say this was a sudden insight on behalf of the pope to "open up the windows to let in fresh air." But there had been a long series of thorough studies that pointed to the need for renewal within the Church about its own identity and self-understanding in the contemporary world. In other words, the council was called to seek ways to inspire and encourage the Church, in all its members, to rediscover itself and the wisdom of its long tradition in light of the challenges of the modern world.

THE "CHURCH" IS PEOPLE

In 1994, St. John Paul II encouraged the Catholic Church to get ready for the new millennium by renewing itself by implementing the teachings of the Second Vatican Council in the life of each Christian as well as in the life of the whole Church (see *On the Coming of the Third Millennium,* 20). All the key teachings of that council grew out of a fundamental "reminder" that the Church as a whole lives from and for Jesus' revelation of God's Spirit. The council was not intent on teaching the members of the Church that God's revelation in Scripture can safely be found and contained in precise, once-and-for-all set doctrines about God and memorized concepts of "how to live." No, the Second Vatican Council wanted us to rediscover that God's will continues to reveal itself to the Church and every one of us in it.

Faith and baptism into the community leads the Christian to recognize that "Church" is people. In every generation, we receive and live

CNS/GREGORY A. SHEMITZ

God's Word in the complexity and limitations of human history. With the pope and the bishops, we are all called to listen for and serve God's word in Scripture and in the tradition handed on to us by previous generations. In this, we each— whether bishop, priest, or layperson—partake in, learn from, and teach each other about a relationship in which faith, holiness, saints, devotions, Mass, service, and mission are but mirrors and facets of God's life in us.

"Communio"

The Church is primarily a "communio," a communion of believers who are members of the body of Christ. While there are many and varied dimensions of the Church, as we saw in the introduction, the foundational reality for all of these is that the Church is a community and communion of believers who share a relationship unlike any other relationship: one that connects us beyond time and place with holy men and women, living and deceased, who are walking with us, marked "with the sign of faith" (First Eucharistic Prayer).

In communio, everyone participates in having the Church become more conformed to the image of Christ (Romans 8:29), and this means that the primary focus is not so much "who does what" or "how many good deeds" we do or don't do; of primary importance is the *quality* with which we love and respect each other. The call to holiness through the Church is best expressed in the way we—as Church—truly listen, proclaim, and respect each other. The mission of the Church is the mission of God's people as a whole.

Evangelization

Many popes since St. John XXIII have spoken about the mission of the Church to share the good news of Jesus Christ through evangelization. Pope Francis summarized this mission in the first year of his pontificate:

The joy of the gospel fills the hearts and lives of all who encounter Jesus. ...[E]ach of us should find ways to communicate Jesus wherever we are. All of us are called to offer others an explicit witness to the saving love of the Lord, who despite our imperfections offers us his closeness, his word and his strength, and gives meaning to our lives.

EVANGELII GAUDIUM (JOY OF THE GOSPEL)

Jesus' Mission

Jesus' goal was to disclose God's love, grace, mercy, forgiveness, and desire to share the divine life with us. This happened in a historical person through historical events that have universal and timeless significance: "Whoever sees me sees him who sent me" (John 12:45).

THE UNIVERSAL CALL TO HOLINESS

Christ glorified is present to us in the Church
through the Holy Spirit to realize in us—
through grace—what he himself is by nature.
The sacraments that the Church celebrates are
the mysteries that reveal the innermost meaning
of the world and bring it to light.

WORSHIP

In the Church's liturgy we identify with the
mysteries in the life of Christ, and we "put on"
Christ in a surrender to God the Father, we
experience God's loving response, we intercede
for others with the Father, and we unite
ourselves to each other in the power of the Holy
Spirit. The root meaning of the word *liturgy*
is "public work." For Catholics, the liturgy is
"the participation of the People of God in 'the

work of God'" (*Catechism of the Catholic Church*, 1069). Our liturgical participation is public, never private. And, not only do we celebrate with the people around us, we are joined by angels and saints and all those who have gone before us praising God in the liturgy of heaven.

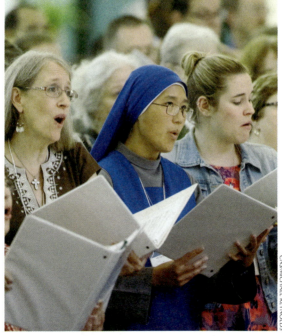

CNS/MICHAEL REYNOLDS

SHARING THE MINISTRY OF CHRIST

All Christians share the ministry of Christ. Saint Paul VI wrote in 1965:

> *In the church, there is diversity of ministry but unity of mission. To the apostles and their successors, Christ has entrusted the office of teaching, sanctifying and governing in his name and by his power. Lay people too, sharing in the priestly, prophetical and kingly office of Christ, play their part in the mission of the whole people of God in the church and in the world.*
>
> DECREE ON THE APOSTOLATE OF LAITY, 2

CNS/GREGORY A. SHEMITZ

Pope Francis echoes this in Joy of the Gospel. This ministry of Christ is not something certain individuals among us have—it is what the Church is! The primary responsibility of a bishop is to evangelize his local Church; the primary responsibility of a layperson is to evangelize his or her own family, workplace, local culture, and political life.

This mission is threefold. The community of believers must:

- Proclaim in word and sacrament that God's reign has come to us in the person of Jesus of Nazareth

- Be "proof" or validation that the reign of God is present and operative in lives of justice, peace, and joy

- Be a challenge to societies and cultures by transforming ourselves according to these principles

Without somehow witnessing to these principles in our lives, our proclamation of God's good news in Jesus Christ is hollow and hypocritical.

THE CHURCH IS THE BEGINNING OF THE KINGDOM OF HEAVEN

The life-giving Spirit of God is the creative force in the creation stories in Genesis. At Pentecost—which is the culmination of the Incarnation, death, resurrection, and ascension of Christ—the same Spirit who was at work at the creation of the world, hovers over a small group of Jesus' disciples and brings forth the seeds of a new creation, a new world, a new human community: the Church.

The Church can only be understood in light of the message Jesus brought: "The time is fulfilled, and the kingdom of God has come near" (Mark 1:15). To have the Spirit poured out on the Christian community means to be in contact with the risen Lord, and this in turn means to be living in the sphere of God's new creation. This means that the Church is the instrument of the still awaited fulfillment of God's reign, the sign of a true yet still imperfect realization of it: The Church "is, on earth, the seed and the beginning of [the] kingdom" (the

Dogmatic Constitution on the Church [*Lumen Gentium*], 5).

In this way, the Church's union with Christ makes it the visible manifestation of the divine reality and presence in our world. As we saw above, the Church is  not identical with this presence, but the Church offers, in an initial way, the fulfillment of human destiny through proclaiming, in time and history, God's plan for the world. Only by seeing itself as a historical sign that points beyond itself can the Church accomplish its mission to lead all humanity toward its final destiny.

NANCY BAUER/SHUTTERSTOCK

SPACE EVOKES COMMUNITY

There is an indispensable bond between the Christian revelation and the spaces in which we celebrate this vision and hope. Church buildings are places where space evokes our thoughts and feelings about what it means to be part of this community, where "gazing accompanies hearing, silence unites with gesture, touch is embraced by scent, and the possible, visible, gives way to the impossible, invisible, as worshipers are engaged in an antiphonal dialogue of private and public experience…a 'human space' indicative of society's quality of life" (Timothy J. Johnson, *Out From the Shadows: Bonaventure's Minor Legend of Saint Francis and the Franciscan Production of Space,* Unpublished manuscript, 2002).

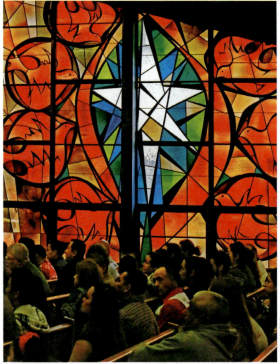

BILL WITTMAN

Conclusion

There has never been a "Church-less" period since the words of Christ on Holy Thursday: "Do this in remembrance of me." These words refer obviously to the Eucharist, but they refer as well to what the Eucharist is all about: creating a people who, in thanksgiving and healing, lives—does—the life of Jesus, pouring itself out in a sacrifice of remembrance and imitation of Christ that transforms our own powerlessness into a new creation in God's image and likeness. The accumulated wisdom of the Church helps us realize that faith in God and relationship with God is also about a God who tells us who we really are and what our deepest meaning, needs, and desires truly are!

Through the presence of the Spirit of Christ the Church is one, holy, catholic, and apostolic. It comprises both divine and human elements. Challenges and crises of faith and leadership are encountered, as are blessings of faith and leadership. The Church is "incarnate" in the world of human beings, and the journey is not yet over.